History of American Holidays

A Thought-Provoking Glimpse into America
Second Edition

Jeff Bensch

Copyright © 2020 Jeffrey Bensch

All rights reserved. No part of this book may be reproduced or used in any form or any means or manner without written permission of the copyright owner except for the use of quotations in a book review.

To request permissions, contact the publisher at jeffbensch@yahoo.com

Second Edition August 2021

ISBN 978-1-7359673-4-9 (hardcover)

ISBN 978-1-7359673-5-6 (paperback - color)

ISBN 978-1-7359673-6-3 (paperback - b/w)

ISBN 978-1-7359673-7-0 (ebook)

Library of Congress Control Number: 2021918288

Published by Jeff Bensch
www.jeffbensch.com

Interior design by Mary Neighbour
Cover design by Andrew Neighbour

Images by iStock, Adobe Stock, Flickr, and Common Domain. Wizard of Oz illustration by W.W. Denslow (1900)

The publisher and the author have researched to ensure that the information in this book was accurate and correct at press time, and while this publication is designed to provide accurate information in regard to the subject matter covered, the publisher and the author assume no responsibility for errors, inaccuracies, omissions, or any other inconsistencies herein and hereby disclaim any liability to any party for any loss, damages, or disruption of any kind caused by errors or omissions, whether such errors or omissions result from negligence, accident, or any other cause.

To Mom and Dad

*And to everyone who touches our lives.
Maybe you know who you are,
maybe you don't.*

Table of Contents

Foreword vii

Introduction xi

Happy New Year 1

Martin Luther King Day 7

Valentine's Day 13

Washington's Birthday (Presidents' Day) 19

Easter, Passover, and Spring Observances 27

Mother's Day 31

Memorial Day 37

Juneteenth 41

Father's Day 53

Fourth of July 59

Labor Day 75

Columbus Day/Indigenous Peoples' Day 87

Halloween 95

Veterans Day 101

Thanksgiving 107

Christmas 121

Sources of Inspiration 129

Appendix 131

Contents in Chronological Order

Happy New Year	2000 BCE
Easter, Passover, and Other Spring Observances	33
Christmas	336
Valentine's Day	500
Halloween	700
Fourth of July	1776
Thanksgiving	1863
Memorial Day	1868
Washington's Birthday (Presidents' Day)	1880
Labor Day	1894
Mother's Day	1914
Veterans Day	1919
Columbus Day[*]	1937
Father's Day	1972
Martin Luther King Day	1983
Juneteenth	2021

---

* In 2021, President Biden issued a proclamation recognizing October 11, 2021, as Indigenous Peoples' Day concurrently with Columbus Day.

Foreword

As a small business owner, I needed to stay in contact with clients, suppliers, and other associates. Quarterly newsletters are a common solution, as are online services to help generate content and distribute friendly reminders that our business still exists. I wanted to do something easy and different. Holiday e-mails were the answer. The frequency was right, and it was easy enough to wish people well on each occasion.

The original intent was to provide a brief historical tidbit about the holiday, followed by a notable quote to ponder or inspire. This grew to longer historical accounts, followed by the holiday's importance to America today, and of course, more quotes. I found that people liked the brief accounts of history. Based on the feedback, it was enjoyable to see that I was making history accessible. After nearly ten years, I decided to distill the emails into a book where each chapter is devoted to an American holiday.

I wanted to create a book that focuses on the stories, with the dates provided as supporting details. The stories tie into things that Americans already know, but they may not understand the *why* of the stories—and how they relate to the present day. Each chapter is intended to leave the reader something to ponder about today's America.

I would like this book to create an appreciation of history for everyone. History is fascinating because of real people and their choices, while memorizing dates and taking tests can make history less enjoyable. As Americans, we should know our history and realize that understanding and celebrating our history is essential to our cultural identity. I hope this book reveals a sliver of history that entices people to explore more deeply into the facts and expand beyond the boundaries of the stories presented.

Countless people helped to bring this book together, and I am forever grateful. First there are friends of the business who provided encouraging comments over the years. Then there are the reviewers who took the time to read various versions of the draft manuscript: Sue Murphy, John Good Smith, Sean Cain, and Tim Worley. Cover and

Foreword

layout were created by MediaNeighbours, with images by Marissa Frederick. Publishing a book is no easy task, and the people at MediaNeighbours deserve the credit for getting this book from a draft manuscript to the bookstore shelf or to the e-store webpage.

Introduction

American holidays are more than just a day off work. Each holiday has a special history and meaning, whether they celebrate our defining moments, religious events, historical figures, or seasonal changes. Most Americans understand that Memorial Day is a three-day weekend to start the summer, while Labor Day is a three-day weekend at the end of summer. The history and significance of United States holidays represent much more, as they reflect our cultural identity. Holidays tell a story of who we are and what we value as Americans.

Americans are unique. We are not bonded together by a common geographic origin. We are not bonded by a common race. We are not bonded by a common religion. Americans are bonded by values. We are bonded by the freedom to have independent ideas and the freedom to express those ideas. We are unified by the acceptance of others.

History of American Holidays

We are the greatest societal experiment of humankind. We celebrate the continuing success of this great experiment through our holidays.

Holidays are about uniting Americans. Whether you are conservative or liberal; male, female, or non-binary; Christian, Jewish, Muslim, or Hindu; Native American, black, white, Asian, or Hispanic; northern, southern, eastern, or western; or a Lakers, Red Sox, or Cowboys fan—holidays allow us an opportunity to put all those differences aside and remember that we are all Americans.

Warfare and competition can blind us to those outside our given community, where allegiances are ingrained over long periods of time, making it difficult to think outside the box and see the other side. Holidays allow us an opportunity to be inside the same box, find common ground, and remember what we, as Americans, truly value. Holiday traditions grow from the family, the schools, the towns, the states, to the United States.

This book starts with New Year's Day and journeys through the year to Christmas, retelling the history of each holiday in just enough depth to learn something new and to remember the significance of why Americans commemorate the day. May the stories bring back pleasant memories from younger years and special times in your life.

Introduction

May moments of gratitude fill your spirit as you realize that we are all proud to be Americans.

Happy New Year!

People have been partying on New Year's since it was first observed in ancient Babylon about 4,000 years ago. The Babylonian New Year began with the first new moon after the vernal equinox (first day of spring, in March). In a similar fashion, the Chinese New Year is celebrated with the second new moon following the winter solstice. Each of these makes sense because they are based on the moon. Is January 1st based on the moon, or is it now just ten days after the winter solstice?

Early Roman calendars, circa 800 BCE (before the common era), began the new year at the vernal equinox. These calendars were not perfect and ultimately fell out of sync with the sun. In 46 BCE, Julius Caesar brought together astronomers and mathematicians to create a calendar that is close to what we have today. The Julian calendar was updated by Pope Gregory XIII in 1582. The Gregorian calendar corrected a slight error in the

Julian calendar by eliminating leap years in years divisible by 100, except when divisible by 400. This resulted in a calendar that is still off by 26 seconds per year, and by the year 4909 it will be off by a full day.

Julius Caesar started the year on January 1 to honor the month's namesake: Janus, the Roman god of beginnings, whose two faces allowed him to look back into the past and forward into the future. This concept continues as each year we use this time to look back and see what was and to look forward to see what will be. It is also a time to celebrate another trip around the sun.

Looking back allows us a chance to reflect on personal accomplishments and societal progress. Reflecting on accomplishments, family growth, career progress, and other things of importance provides an opportunity to recognize how high we have climbed. It is a time to look back, see the view, and find gratitude. As a society, we find it interesting to reflect on the big news events and significant pop-culture moments.

Resolutions for the New Year are an enjoyable way to plan and make improvements. For many, however, New Year's resolutions typically last a few days to a few weeks. Here are two unique approaches to New Year's resolutions:

- The One-Word Resolution (Gretchen Rubin).** These are easy to remember and therefore easy to keep. Only one word. Don't over do it. Examples include: diet, sleep, exercise, love, attitude, job, volunteer, adventure, and the list goes on.

- Make a Plan on January 1st. Whether it's to take a vacation or a class, join an organization, or begin a new activity, just decide on January 1st. Then on January 2nd, set the date, reserve the hotel, buy the ticket, invite your family and friends, and set it up to happen. Look forward to it in the coming months and be ready when the date arrives. Resolution accomplished.

Celebrations take on many forms throughout the world. Many of these celebrations have made their way to the United States and have a part in our traditions. Making noise with party horns and sirens dates back to firecrackers in China, church

---

** Authors these days have so many venues of distribution. From their books, websites, and calendars; to podcasts and blogs, sometimes it is difficult to appropriately reference where an idea originated. Nonetheless, Rubin has a seemingly endless supply of good ideas.

bells in Italy, and the early American colonists shooting pistols. Foods and beverages are also traditional. We enjoy a range of drinks from champagne to punch-bowl favorites, and we feast on traditional foods. In the southern United States, a dish of black-eyed peas and pork in a stew (*Good Luck Hoppin' John*) is enjoyed both for its taste and to provide good fortune throughout the year. Other traditional activities include cleaning the house, watching parades, and cheering college football teams on New Year's Day.

Looking ahead to the new year, the future is always bright. The economic outlook is good, world peace is on the horizon, and it is a time for self-improvement. Healthy lifestyle theories and recommendations evolve, and today we are learning that diet, exercise, meditation, and sleep are the best doctors. At the same time, we know that professional doctors are available when the "best doctors" are not enough. With that in mind, health care will continue to improve, as will almost every problem in front of us today.

Most importantly, there will be plenty of opportunities for everyone. As Americans, we fix the problems in front of us. The wonder of freedom in America is that you can do almost anything you want. The problem is that you cannot do everything you want. Use your time wisely and work together to solve the world's problems. This is going to be the best year ever.

Happy New Year!

Quotes to Ponder

Be at war with your vices, at peace with your neighbors, and let every New Year find you a better man.
    Benjamin Franklin

Learn from yesterday, live for today, hope for tomorrow.
    Albert Einstein

Enjoy the process because the journey is often better than the destination.
    Anonymous

Finish each day [year] and be done with it. You have done what you could; some blunders and absurdities have crept in; forget them as soon as you can. Tomorrow is a new day [year]; you shall begin it serenely and with too high a spirit to be encumbered with your old nonsense.
　　　　　　　　　Ralph Waldo Emerson

Martin Luther King Day

Martin Luther King Day has come to be known as MLK Weekend for many people. For some, it is a busy ski weekend, although for others we miss the times when our children were in grade school, and we would get a dose of MLK history at this time of year. There are also the radio stations playing parts of Dr. King's great speeches for a few minutes each year. Dr. Martin Luther King's life was full of struggles and accomplishments beyond compare. Here are a few interesting facts that we tend to forget after high school:

- Born January 15, 1929, in Atlanta, Georgia
- Gifted student. Skipped the 9th and 12th grades

- Started college at age 15 and graduated in 1948 from Morehouse College in Atlanta
- Graduated from Crozer Theological Seminary, near Philadelphia, in 1951
- PhD in theology from Boston University in 1955
- Led the Montgomery Bus Boycott later in 1955, following Rosa Parks's refusal to give up her bus seat
- Survived a murder attempt when stabbed at a book signing in 1958
- Suffered depression
- Went to prison 29 times
- Non-violent activist inspired by Mahatma Gandhi

- Activist for racial equality, financial equality, and peace
- March on Washington in August 1963; delivered his "I Have a Dream" speech
- Won the Nobel Peace Prize in 1964
- Instrumental in the Civil Rights Act of 1964
- Instrumental in the Voting Rights Act of 1965
- March from Selma to Montgomery, March 1965; delivered his "How Long, Not Long" speech
- Assassinated on April 4, 1968

Source: National Park Service, www.nps.gov/malu

Only four days after King's assassination, Representative John Conyers from Michigan took to the floor of Congress to create a federal holiday for Dr. King. Although the first bill failed, Congressman Conyers presented the bill every year thereafter until it passed 15 years later, in 1983, over the filibuster attempt by Senator Jesse Helms of North Carolina. President Ronald Reagan immediately signed the legislation to celebrate Dr. Martin Luther King's birthday, although it was not until 2000 that every state recognized the holiday. Like so many things in American politics, change takes time. Although we have come a long way from 1968, we are not nearly as far along as we would like. We just strive to keep moving forward.

Quotes to Ponder

Everywhere you look for quotes, many of the best are from Dr. Martin Luther King. Here are a few favorites:

> *Injustice anywhere is a threat to justice everywhere.*
>
> *Darkness cannot drive out Darkness; only Light can do that.*
> *Hate cannot drive out Hate; only Love can do that.*

Martin Luther King Day

*The Negro needs the white man
to free him from his fears.
The white man needs the Negro
to free him from his guilt.*

*Even though we face the difficulties
of today and tomorrow,
I still have a dream. It is a dream
rooted in the American dream.*

Valentine's Day

In ancient Rome, during the festival of Lupercus, the god of fertility, the priests would sacrifice goats to the god. They would then run through the streets of Rome carrying pieces of the goat skin. To be struck by the skin would enhance fertility. Young women would come forth to be struck and young men would draw names for "blind dates" during the coming year.

The day is named after one or more early Christian martyrs named Valentine. One legend says the Roman Emperor outlawed marriage for all young men, to make them better soldiers. Valentine defied the Emperor and continued to perform marriages for young couples. Once imprisoned, Valentine wrote letters from prison to his beloved before his death. He signed the letters, "From your Valentine." The feast of St. Valentine was established by Pope Gelasius I in 500 CE (common era).

Valentine's Day became associated with romantic love based on a story by Geoffrey Chaucer ("The Parliament of Fowls," 1381), which includes these lines:

> *[S]o this goddess surpasses all other creatures in beauty. . . . [H]igh upon a hill covered in flowers, the noble goddess Nature was sitting. Her halls and chambers were the branches and boughs of trees . . . and there was not a single bird born of a mother that was not sitting attentively before her, to hear what she had to say and to receive its fortune, for this was Saint Valentine's Day, and every bird was there to choose its mate.*

Valentine's Day

The tradition of gift giving on Valentine's Day has existed for centuries. Valentine's Day cards date back to 1415, when love notes were sent by Charles, Duke of Orleans, while a prisoner in the Tower of London. By the 16th century, several religious leaders preached against card giving. Love cannot be stopped, however, and cards were first mass produced in 1847 by Esther A. Howland, whose father operated a book and stationary store in Worcester, Massachusetts. In 1969, Pope Paul VI deleted Valentine's Day from the Roman calendar of saints, to reduce the number of saint days of legendary origin. Nonetheless, the tradition of love continues.

Today, cards are the most common way to show your love on Valentine's Day, with an estimated 180 million cards exchanged during the holiday. Roses were established as a tradition in the 17th century, because they are supposedly the favorite flower of Venus, the Roman goddess of love. It was the 16th century when Spanish conquistadors brought chocolate from Mexico back to the Old World, and it became the dessert of choice because of its aphrodisiac effects. Today, Amcricans spend nearly $20 billion each Valentine's Day, or more than $150 per person taking part in the celebrations.

Valentine's Day gift-giving, however, has perplexed many. What's the appropriate way to express love to that special someone? After many years of experience, and as a gift to all gift-giving-challenged friends, here are a few rules for Valentine's Day gifts:

1. Leftover Christmas chocolate – doesn't work;

2. Flowers – 100 percent success rate;

3. Practical gifts – good grief, and good luck;

4. Specialty gift – return and exchange likely; and

5. Cards with a handwritten message from the heart – 100 percent success rate.

Valentine's Day

Quotes to Ponder

If you are at a loss for words for that heartfelt message, here are a few quotes to get things started:

If I know what love is, it is because of you.
Herman Hesse

I know no greater happiness than to be with you all the time, without interruption, without end.
Franz Kafka

Being deeply loved by someone gives you strength, while loving someone deeply gives you courage.
Lao Tzu

Love is composed of a single soul inhabiting two bodies.
Aristotle

A kiss is a lovely trick designed by nature to stop speech when words become superfluous.
Ingrid Bergman

All you need is love.
Lennon-McCartney

All you need is love, but a little chocolate now and then doesn't hurt.
Charles Schulz

Washington's Birthday (Presidents' Day)

Is it President's Day, Presidents' Day, or is it George Washington's Birthday? The possessive apostrophe for one president could be incorrect because most of us agree that this day celebrates Washington's birthday (February 22) and Abraham Lincoln's birthday (February 12). Some understand this day to celebrate all United States Presidents. In these cases, Presidents' Day is correct.

George Washington's Birthday has been celebrated since 1800; it officially became a federal holiday in 1880. Abraham Lincoln's Birthday was celebrated following his death, by a number of states as a legal holiday, but it has never been a federal holiday largely due to opposition from Southern states during and after Reconstruction.

In 1968 Congress passed the *Uniform Monday Holiday Bill* and moved the Washington's Birthday observance to the third Monday in February. This incurred objections from those believing that the federal holidays should be celebrated on the true historical date, while others endorsed moving observances to Mondays, to create three-day weekends. The bill took effect in 1971, and the day is still officially known as Washington's Birthday.

The term "Presidents' Day" began appearing publicly in the 1980s. Approximately a dozen state governments officially renamed their Washington's Birthday observances to "Presidents' Day," "Washington's and Lincoln's Day," or other such designations. Some city and county governments still observe both days as holidays. By the way, only two other presidents have February birthdays: Ronald Reagan and William Henry Harrison.

George Washington, as one of our founding fathers, led the birth of our nation from the battlefields against the British, to becoming the first president of the United States. As the first president, he established the federal judiciary and the United States Navy. More importantly, after being the leader of the military and serving two terms in office, President Washington abided by the rules of a new nation and stepped down without assuming extraordinary or extended powers.

Washington's Birthday (Presidents' Day)

The founding fathers established the balance of powers, and George Washington set the standard for all future presidents.

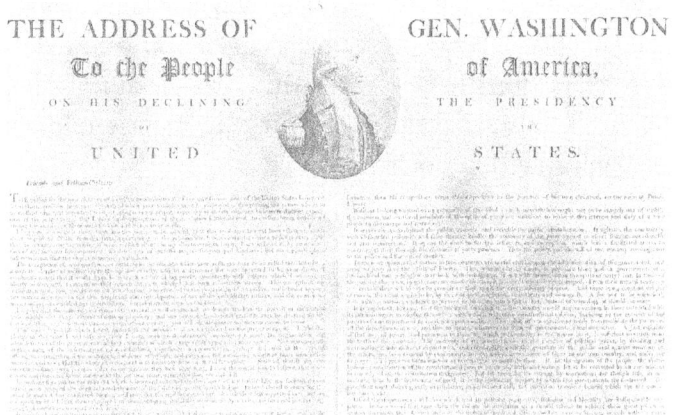

Did you know that every year on February 22 the Senate listens to a reading of George Washington's Farewell Address? In it, President Washington advised American citizens to view themselves as a cohesive unit and avoid excessive political party spirit and geographical distinctions. In foreign affairs, he warned against long-term alliances with other nations. What will be going through the minds of our senators this year as they listen to the words of George Washington from 1796?

President Lincoln led our nation through the Civil War—a war against slavery, a war against economic separation, a war to preserve our unity in the 1860s. President Lincoln also established the federal banking system with a national currency, the first versions of the internal revenue service, and the land-grant college system. At the end of the day, however, Lincoln is remembered for the Civil War, ending slavery (Emancipation Proclamation), and beginning the healing process (Reconstruction). From the battlefield of Gettysburg he spoke:

> [F]rom these honored dead we take increased devotion to that cause for which they gave the last full measure of devotion—
> that we here highly resolve that these dead shall not have died in vain—
> that this nation, under God, shall have a new birth of freedom—
> and that government of the people, by the people, for the people, shall not perish from the earth.

What about today? Some say we are in the midst of the greatest political turmoil of all time. Is that a matter of perspective? Consider that in the 20th century we witnessed the Iran-Contra scandal, Watergate, the Vietnam War, and two World Wars. For illumination, let's return to 1900, more than 100 years ago, with the great modern fairy tale, *The Wonderful Wizard of Oz* by L. Frank Baum. The story, intentionally or unintentionally, satirizes our political system and applauds the strength and spirit of the average American.

Washington's Birthday (Presidents' Day)

We have Dorothy (American people/values), naïve and honest, trying to find her way home, assisting the Scarecrow (American farmers and laborers), who is out of work and ideas, the Tin Man (industrial workers), rusted with factory shutdowns and

Original illustration by W. W. Denslow, downloaded from the Library of Congress.

unemployment, and the cowardly Lion (Congress), with a lot of talk and little action. Together they travel the yellow brick road (gold, money) to seek their salvation at the Emerald City (Washington, DC), seeking solutions to their problems from the Wizard of Oz.

The Great Oz pretends to be benevolent, wise, and powerful, when in fact he is a selfish fraud. He sends Dorothy into severe danger to conquer *his* enemy, the Wicked Witch of the West (American Western frontier in the 1890s) along with her winged monkeys (Native Americans). When the West is civilized, and Dorothy returns to Emerald City, the Great Oz is exposed as the fraud that he is by Dorothy's little dog, Toto (average Americans). Being exposed, Oz provides shallow, questionable honors to keep Dorothy, Scarecrow, Tin Man, and the Lion happy. And that my friends . . . is a horse of a different color.

Quotes to Ponder

How do you talk if you don't have a brain?
        Dorothy

Well, some people without brains do an awful lot of talking, don't they?
        Scarecrow

Washington's Birthday (Presidents' Day)

Pay no attention to that man behind the curtain.
> The Great Oz

Once we were a free people, living happily in the great forest . . . doing just as we pleased, without calling anybody master. . . . This was many years ago, long before Oz came out of the clouds to rule over this land.
> King of the Winged Monkeys,
> *The Wonderful Wizard of Oz* (book)

More Quotes to Ponder

To balance that satire, here are a few great presidential quotes:

There is nothing which can better deserve our patronage than the promotion of science and literature. Knowledge is in every country the surest basis of public happiness.
> George Washington, 1st President
> of the United States of America

America will never be destroyed from the outside. If we falter and lose our freedoms, it will be because we destroyed ourselves.
> Abraham Lincoln, 16th President
> of the United States of America

The only legitimate right to govern is an express grant of power from the governed.
William Henry Harrison, 9th President
of the United States of America

There are no constraints on the human mind, no walls around the human spirit, no barriers to our progress except those we ourselves erect.
Ronald Reagan, 40th President
of the United States of America

Easter, Passover, and Spring Observances

When you were a child, did you ever ask your parents, "When is Easter?" Most parents would have to look at a calendar. Maybe you asked, "Why is Easter on a different day every year?" or "Do bunnies lay eggs?"

Many Christian parents would likely say that Easter is the Sunday after Good Friday. They may not realize that Easter is the first Sunday, after the first full moon, after the northern spring equinox (March 21). Therefore, Easter can be as early

as March 22, or as late as April 25, depending on the lunar cycles. If you are looking to set records, Easter will be on March 22 in 2285 and on April 25 in 2038.

Many Jewish parents probably understand that Easter is related to the Jewish holiday of Passover, celebrating the exodus of the Jews from slavery in Egypt. Passover is a seven-day holiday that begins on the 15th day of the month of Nisan, from the Hebrew calendar, which is usually the first full moon after the northern hemisphere spring equinox.

The Last Supper of Jesus and his twelve apostles was a Passover feast that occurred on the Thursday night prior to Jesus's arrest and crucifixion on Good Friday. Easter Sunday then observes the resurrection of Jesus Christ on the third day following his death. Through this, Jesus Christ, Son of God, suffered for mankind's sins and God provided eternal life to all who accept Jesus as their savior.

> *Jesus told her, "I am the resurrection and the life. Anyone who believes in me will live, even after dying."*
> John 11:25-26

The origins of Easter also date back to ancient spring rituals from Germanic paganism (Teutonic mythology). Derived from the name Eostre, the Anglo-Saxon goddess of spring, the festivals celebrated the spring equinox and the return of light and sunshine from the depths of winter.

Because early English Christians wanted other northern Europeans to accept Christianity, they decided to use the name Easter to increase comfort levels and encourage acceptance. Toward that end, they also adopted some pagan rituals that remain today: Easter eggs represent fertility, while the Easter Bunny is associated with new life and rebirth of the seasons.

Whether it is religious significance or a celebration of the seasons, Easter, Passover, and the spring season provide a time for reflection and renewal. With family activities, work, and living life to the fullest, Easter provides a time to review and appreciate our existence today and into the future.

Quotes to Ponder

Our Lord has written the promise of resurrection, not in books alone, but in every leaf in springtime.
   Martin Luther, 16th-century
   Christian theologian

The day which we fear as our last is but the birthday of eternity.
   Seneca, Roman philosopher

Life can only be understood backwards; but it must be lived forwards.
   Soren Kierkegaard, 19-century
   Danish philosopher

Die happily and look forward to taking up a new and better form. Like the sun, only when you set in the west can you rise in the east.
   Jelaluddin Rumi, 13th-century
   Persian poet

When you are born, you cry, and the world rejoices. When you die, you rejoice, and the world cries.
   Buddhist saying

The days are long, but the years are short.
   Gretchen Rubin, *The Happiness Project*

Mother's Day

The history of Mother's Day has roots in Greek and Roman mythology, as well as the Christian 16th-century festival known as Mothering Sunday. In the United States, Mother's Day began in the 1800s, as mothers worked together to improve the lives of their children.

The Greek goddess Rhea is considered the mother of the gods. She is the daughter of Gaia (Mother Earth) and Ouranos (Father Sky). Greek mythology worships Rhea for her comfort and ease, as the supreme mother of the gods. She was married to Cronus, who heard the prophecy that one of his children would overthrow him. Cronus decided to swallow each child shortly after birth to prevent this prophecy. Rhea, however, was able to hide Zeus and gave Cronus a rock wrapped in a blanket to swallow. Zeus was raised in hiding and, as an adult, mixed a potion that Cronus drank,

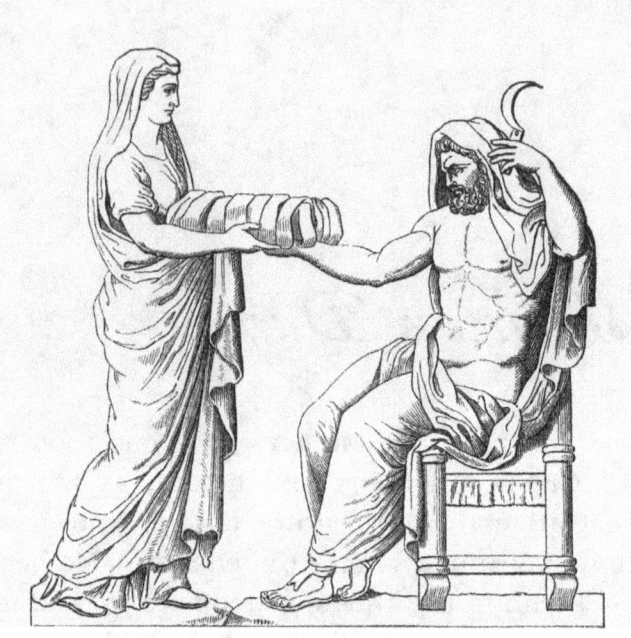
Rhea and Cronos

causing him to vomit all of his children back to life. Zeus eventually did overthrow Cronus and fulfilled the prophecy.

Cybele is the great-mother goddess of ancient Rome. She was brought to Rome near the end of the third century BCE, to help defeat Carthage in the Second Punic War. Victory against Carthage and an end to the famine brought Rome into prominence. In what may be considered the first Mother's Day celebrations, the Roman Megalesia festival to the Magna Mater (Great Mother) began in 191 BCE with annual celebrations on April 4, commemorating the date of Cybele's arrival in Rome.

In the 16th-century, Christians in the United Kingdom and Ireland practiced a return to the church of their baptism during Lent. If their "mother church" was too far away, the local parish was acceptable. This grew into a time for families to gather and visit the church together. This evolved further into the holiday Mothering Sunday, when servants would get the day off to attend with their own mothers and children. Through the centuries, Mothering Sunday included giving gifts to mothers, although the holiday began to wane until it was revived in the early 1900s. Today it is celebrated on the fourth Sunday during Lent by the Church of England and the Church of Ireland.

In the United States, Mother's Day originated before the Civil War, in the 1850s, when Ann Reeves Jarvis from West Virginia held Mother's Day work clubs to improve sanitary conditions to lower infant mortality. The groups also tended wounded soldiers from both sides during the Civil War, and organized picnics and other events to unite former foes after the war. This post-Civil War recovery is very similar to the origins of Memorial Day, although Mother's Day had more of an activist side, as is evident in the *Mother's*

Day Proclamation, written in 1870 by Julia Ward Howe, where she asks all women to join the political process:

> As men have often forsaken the plow and the anvil at the summons of war, let women now leave all that may be left of home for a great and earnest day of counsel. . . . Let them then solemnly take counsel with each other as to the means whereby the great human family can live in peace, each bearing . . . the sacred impress, not of Caesar, but of God.

Julia Ward Howe was an accomplished author, abolitionist, and suffragist in the 1800s. From her days in the 1840s hanging out with the likes of Ralph Waldo Emerson and Henry Wadsworth Longfellow, to writing "The Battle Hymn of the Republic," Ms. Howe championed the freedom of slaves and women's right to vote. She supported the 15th Amendment giving black men the right to vote in 1870, and she founded numerous suffrage associations, including the American Woman Suffrage Association (1869) that later merged with Susan B. Anthony's rival organization, the National Woman Suffrage Association (NWSA) in 1890. Ms. Howe died in 1910, however, and did not live to see passage of the 19th Amendment on August 18, 1920, giving women the right to vote.

Mother's Day

It wasn't until Ann Reeves Jarvis died in 1905 that her daughter Anna Jarvis was inspired to organize the first modern-era Mother's Day observances, in 1908. This grew with the help of Mr. John Wanamaker, a department-store owner in Philadelphia. Anna's efforts continued, and she was adamant in honoring each person's most important mother in the world—their own. In 1914 President Woodrow Wilson officially established the second Sunday in May as Mother's Day. The commercialism of Mother's Day, however, irritated Anna Jarvis, and she fought relentlessly for the rest of her life to eliminate this aspect of the holiday.

Mother's Day celebrations in the United States are officially more than 100 years running. It is one of the largest spending holidays of the year, averaging nearly $170 per mother, totaling nearly $20 billion. Mother's Day is clearly more than just money and gifts. More phone calls are made each Mother's Day than any other day of the year. Whether we are calling our mothers or our children, the never-ending appreciation first recognized by Greek mythology endures today.

Quotes to Ponder

God could not be everywhere, and therefore he made mothers.
Rudyard Kipling

Life doesn't come with a manual. It comes with a mother.
Unknown

A mother's hug lasts long after she lets go.
Unknown

Motherhood is the biggest gamble in the world. It is the glorious life force. It's huge and scary—it's an act of infinite optimism.
Gilda Radner

Memorial Day

Memorial Day is a day of remembrance for those who died in battle for our country. It is interesting that this day of remembrance began somewhat spontaneously and separately in towns across regions devastated by the Civil War. Mothers and wives of fallen soldiers started gatherings in the 1860s to honor those who had died.

Congressman and former general John Alexander Logan proclaimed on May 5, 1868, that Memorial Day would be observed on May 30 each year, and flowers were placed on the graves of Union and Confederate soldiers at Arlington National Cemetery. The South did not recognize the official Memorial Day until after World War I, when it was changed from honoring those who died in the Civil War to honoring those Americans who died in any war. Memorial Day was changed from May 30 to the last Monday in May as part of the National Holiday Act of 1971, to assure a three-day weekend. While the three-day weekend is a nice start to summer, many believe this has deteriorated the true meaning of the holiday.

Memorial gatherings, sprung from grief and the need for healing, occurred independently in a time without widely accessible long-distance communication, yet they were similar in their practice.

Memorial Day

After more than 620,000 American casualties in the Civil War, these gatherings were needed for the living to grieve and commemorate loved ones. This death toll represents approximately 2 percent of the total population in 1865, and a much larger part of the male population, ages 18 to 28—not to mention the many wounded who suffered when medical advances were nothing close to what we have today. The Civil War devastated our country, and the effects of war extended beyond the casualties to war-torn generations and reconstruction efforts that still affect our lives today.

To put things in perspective, there were approximately 420,000 American casualties in World War II (0.3 percent of the population), while Germany lost over 5,000,000 soldiers in the war. Of that, Germany lost over 3,500,000 soldiers in Russia, as Hitler was trying to take over the world. WW II was not kind to Russia either, as they lost a staggering 26,000,000 people (nearly 14 percent of their total population).

Some say that Russia defeated Germany and the United States was the beneficiary. If Hitler had understood history and what happened to Napoleon in Russia, who knows? We could all be speaking German today.

History is interesting, even if it may be boring for high school students. Hopefully, our day of remembrance and gratitude does not get lost in the weekend car sales and barbecues.

Quotes to Ponder

Those who have long enjoyed such privileges as we enjoy, forget in time that men have died to win them.
            Franklin D. Roosevelt

We are determined to achieve an enduring peace—a peace with liberty and with honor. This determination, this resolve, is the highest tribute we can pay to the many who have fallen in the service of our Nation.
            Ronald Reagan

As we express our gratitude, we must never forget that the highest appreciation is not to utter the words, but to live by them.
            John F. Kennedy

It is foolish and wrong to mourn the men who died. Rather we should thank God that such men lived.
            George S. Patton

Juneteenth

The last enslaved black Americans were notified of their freedom on June 19, 1865, in Galveston Bay, Texas. In 2021, 156 years later, Juneteenth became an official federal holiday to be celebrated every year on June 19th.

This holiday covers a significant portion of American history, from the Civil War to the civil rights legislation of the 1960s to our continuing evolution as Americans. Although it took more than a century and a half for this holiday to finally be recognized, Juneteenth was one of the quickest holiday approvals by the federal government.

Fast action for something long overdue:

- Tuesday, June 15th, 2021, the bill passed in the US Senate
- Wednesday, June 16th, the House of Representatives passed it

- Thursday, June 17th, President Joseph Biden signed it into law
- Friday, June 18th, federal employees enjoyed the first day off from work in celebration of the holiday
- Saturday, June 19, 2021, became the first, official federal Juneteenth holiday.

While the congressional action may sound fast, it had previously been introduced in Congress in February 2021, as it was in 2020, although it never made it to the floor for a vote in 2020. It was also in 2020 that then President Donald Trump scheduled a rally in Tulsa, Oklahoma, on June 19th, only to reschedule it to June 20th because of the backlash. In one respect, President Trump gave Juneteenth widespread recognition that it did not have, and he did promise in subsequent campaign speeches to make Juneteenth a national holiday.

The signing of the Emancipation Proclamation freed enslaved Americans in 1863, yet it took two more years to free the last slaves in Texas. This may seem like a long time to get the word out, but there was a lot going on – like the Civil War. Texas was a Confederate state and did not recognize the United States government, let alone the Emancipation Proclamation. More realistically, it took two months from the Confederate surrender in April 1865 until the slaves in Texas were notified of their freedom. At the same time, the Thirteenth Constitutional Amendment was passed by the Senate in April 1864, and by the House of Representatives on January 31, 1865, signed by President Lincoln on February 1, 1865, and finally ratified by at least two-thirds of the States in December 1865. It was also later ratified by Texas in 1870.

It is easy to wonder why Juneteenth took so long to become a federal holiday; 156 years is a long time. Three reasons to consider are: first it took a civil war to get things headed in the right direction; second, Reconstruction was a monumental task; and third, the Civil War did not remove the underlying obstacle of racial prejudice. In fact, the Confederate surrender occurred on April 9, 1865, and President Lincoln was assassinated within the week, on April 14, 1865, by John Wilkes Booth, who supported the Confederate cause and the institution of slavery.

Reconstruction

Vice President Andrew Johnson assumed office following Lincoln's assassination. While Lincoln was a Republican, and the Republican party opposed slavery, it was common in the 1800s to have a member of the opposite party as a running mate to expand the ticket's overall appeal. Andrew

Johnson was a rare Democrat who opposed slavery, but he was sympathetic to conditions in the Southern states and weakened numerous attempts to integrate freed slaves into America's economic, political, and social life. As an example, reparations of forty-acres (and a mule), ordered by General William Sherman following his famous march to the sea, was initially a tremendous success, with approximately 400,000 acres distributed to freedmen. From a military perspec-

tive this made perfect sense. General Sherman was probably thinking, "Damn! We won the war, we will take the land and give it to whomever we want." President Johnson, however, overturned this order and returned the lands to their original owners – the same people that had declared war on the United States.

Nonetheless, Reconstruction continued. Congress got busy and passed three amendments to the constitution that were ratified by at least two-thirds of the states:

> The Thirteenth Amendment, 1865, eliminated slave labor except as punishment for a crime.
>
> *
>
> The Fourteenth Amendment, 1868, conferred citizenship upon anyone born in the United States; based representation in Congress upon the full population of each district (including all freedmen); and prohibited any person taking office in Congress, the Senate, or as President and Vice President who has engaged in insurrection or rebellion against the United States (Confederate military and politicians).
>
> *
>
> The Fifteenth Amendment, 1870, provided the right to vote for any man; moreover that right could not "be denied or abridged by the United States, or by any State, on account of race, color, or previous condition of servitude."

With these Amendments, Reconstruction moved forward. More than 600 freedmen were elected to state legislative offices, and a few were elected to Congress. At the same time, however, Black

Codes were being passed in Southern states to limit the rights of black Americans. Black Codes were laws that made it easy to arrest black men for crimes that would fit the "loophole" of the Thirteenth Amendment clause, "except for punishment of a crime." For instance, it was illegal for black men to loiter – so two black men could be arrested if they were found outdoors talking to each other. Black men were required to enter into labor contracts. Without a contract, they could be arrested. It was illegal for a prospective new employer to offer a black man a higher wage than his current employer was paying. Fines could be assessed against black men for various reasons and arrests would follow if the fines could not be paid. If a black man were arrested, his children could be considered orphans, taken into the custody of the state, and be placed in "apprenticeship" programs. In essence, slavery continued.

President Johnson turned a blind eye to the Black Codes, similar to his overturning of the forty-acres-and-a-mule program. Congress, however, passed the Civil Rights Act of 1866, even overriding a presidential veto in the process. Congress also impeached President Johnson, who survived by one vote in the Senate trial following his impeachment.

Through all of this, violence against black Americans in the South continued unpunished. Black women were victimized, and black men were lynched, tortured, and murdered without repercussions from law enforcement. In addition, the Ku Klux Klan gained significant power in Southern states, with a violence-first approach against Republican politicians and outspoken freedmen.

President Johnson did not win a second term, and former Civil War Union General Ulysses S. Grant became the eighteenth president of the United States. Grant reinvigorated Reconstruction by strengthening the Freedmen's Bureau and other federal programs to find fair wages for freedmen, establish schools for black children, and implement economic and social programs for an integrated society. The Ku Klux Klan was pushed back and broadly controlled. The Civil Rights Act of 1875 was also passed under the Grant administration.

The economy began to struggle in the early 1870s, and poverty was relatively widespread. Poor whites in the North were oppressed by management, with low wages and poor living conditions across most industries. Support for Reconstruction began to decline, and the Democratic party took control of the House of Representatives during the mid-term elections of 1874. The disputed presidential election of 1876 was resolved through a compromise that allowed the Republican candidate, Rutherford B. Hayes, to become president in exchange for removing military troops from Southern states. The demise of Reconstruction that began in 1877 was solidified further in 1883, by the Supreme Court decision that declared the Civil Rights Act of 1875 unconstitutional.

Jim Crow to Civil Rights Legislation

Without military control, the Ku Klux Klan and their violence returned to the South, and Jim Crow laws replaced the Black Codes. The Jim Crow laws established segregation as the norm. Blacks were banned from parks, restaurants, schools, restrooms, building entrances, neighborhoods, hospitals, and essentially every other social, economic, or political institution in American society—including, of course, buses. Life was difficult for black Americans through these times. It also was not easy for poor white Americans working in the factories and agricultural fields in the North. More race and labor riots occurred across the country during this time than we care to admit.

At the turn of the twentieth century, Republicans controlled much of the political landscape while allowing Democratic control of Southern states. From presidents Theodore Roosevelt, Warren Harding, Calvin Coolidge, and Herbert Hoover, Republicans opposed slavery, supported isolationism and high tariffs, and were business friendly through the Roaring 20s to the Great

Depression. President Hoover, with unemployment rising above 20 percent, believed that helping the unemployed would create complacency or laziness in the American worker. He also believed that black Americans could improve their place in society with education and personal initiative, and he did nothing to curb Jim Crow laws or support a federal anti-lynching law. Combine this with appointing a Southern judge to the Supreme Court, Hoover paved the way for black Americans to rally behind Democratic presidential candidate Franklin D. Roosevelt in 1938.

The oppression of black Americans continued for generations, with some advances. The United States military was integrated under President Harry S. Truman in 1948. In 1954, the Supreme Court ruled that "separate but equal" was not possible or constitutional in *Brown vs. the Board of Education*. And in 1955, Rosa Parks refused to

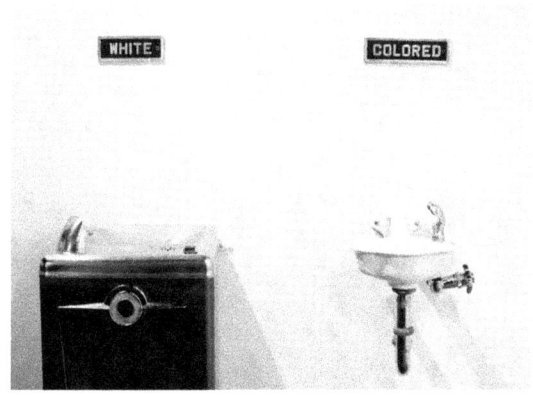

History of American Holidays

give up her bus seat. Congress passed a new Civil Rights Act in 1964, under the Commerce Clause of the Constitution, and they also passed the Voting Rights Act of 1965 and the Fair Housing Act of 1968.

Through all this, America continues to evolve. Although we have come a long way, we are still not where we need to be. Looking back, it has taken far too long: from that day in 1865, when Union General Gordan Granger announced that all black Americans were free, until today, when we recognize Juneteenth as a day of freedom. We now celebrate Juneteenth every year two weeks before we celebrate the United States' freedom on July 4th. If you recognize moving on from the hypocrisy of our past, these holidays now become holidays for all Americans to celebrate together.

Quotes to Ponder

Every year we must remind successive generations that this event triggered a series of events that one by one defines the challenges and responsibilities of successive generations. That's why we need this holiday.

                Former Texas Rep. Al Edwards,
                Father of the Juneteenth Holiday

Father's Day

In the Catholic Church, Saint Joseph's Day honors Joseph, husband of the Virgin Mary and the recognized human father of Jesus Christ. In or around the 10th century, the Church dedicated March 19 to Saint Joseph, while the Eastern Orthodox Catholic Church celebrates Saint Joseph on the first Sunday after Christmas. Customs, festivals, and feasts were established in Rome by the mid-15th-century and eventually became recognized as Father's Day in many Catholic communities. Saint Joseph's Day is still Father's Day in Italy, Spain, and Portugal.

During the Middle Ages, Sicily was suffering a great drought and famine. Prayers to Saint Joseph brought rain and the first crop of fava beans. Joseph became the patron saint of Sicily and of workers. In 1870, Pope Pius IX declared Joseph Patron of the Universal Church. Celebrations on Saint Joseph's Day include giving food to the needy, specifically fava beans and breadcrumbs to represent the dust of a carpenter.

Within the Catholic Church, March 19 was later changed to the third Sunday after Easter, and then moved by Pope Pius X in 1911 to the Wednesday preceding Easter to coincide with the day of the week dedicated to Saint John the Baptist and other local patron saints. The Saint Joseph feasts and celebrations were abolished by Pope Pius XII in 1955, during a modernization of Catholic laws and celebrations. At the same time, Pope Pius XII established a celebration to Saint Joseph the Worker. In 1969, the Feast of Saint Joseph was reduced to an optional memorial, the lowest ranking for a saint's day in the Catholic Church.

In the United States, Father's Day began in 1909, when the daughter of William Jackson Smart thought that her dad deserved special recognition. Sonora Smart Dodd was one of six children raised by Mr. Smart, a widower in Spokane, Washington. Ms. Dodd visited churches, local

establishments, and government officials to garner support, and very quickly the State of Washington celebrated the first official Father's Day on June 19, 1910.

It took a long time for Father's Day to gain nationwide support. In 1916, President Wilson acknowledged the day through telegraph signals that remarkably unfurled a flag in Spokane after he pressed a button in Washington, DC. President Coolidge urged state governments to observe Father's Day in 1924. Ms. Dodd continued to promote the Father's Day holiday through the depression of the 1930s and longer. Father's Day was also supported by business organizations hoping to spur economic activity with dad-related gifts and celebrations. Fathers in general, however, were not overly enthused by a Sunday celebration. Most fathers would have preferred a Friday at the ballpark or a Monday fishing.

It was not until 56 years after the first Father's Day that President Lyndon Johnson issued an executive order, in 1966, and then six years later President Richard Nixon signed a proclamation, in 1972, making the third Sunday in June Father's Day. Today, Father's Day is celebrated around the world in more than 70 countries. More than $1 billion is spent each year on dad-related gifts and celebrations.

Questions remain, however. Why did it take so long to recognize fathers with a national holiday? Why has Saint Joseph's Day dwindled in importance within the Catholic Church? And why do we spend $20 billion on Mother's Day each year and only $1 billion on Father's Day?

Maybe it is because dads were historically recognized as the breadwinners, not needing sentimental recognition. As we have expanded Father's Day traditions, dads in the media have gone from *Andy Griffith* and *Father Knows Best* to *Modern Family* and *The Simpsons*. Have dads really been transformed from the wise and understanding to the foolish and clueless? We hope the media portrayals don't say much about the value of an active male role model in the American family.

Father's Day is here to bring us together as we connect with our dads, sons, husbands, brothers,

and the other men in our lives. Whether it is the cards, the gifts, or just the time together, every dad appreciates being recognized at least one day each year for being the best father in the world.

Quotes to Ponder

A daughter needs a dad to be the standard against which she will judge all men.
    Gregory E. Lang, American Author

When a father gives to his son, both laugh; when a son gives to his father, both cry.
    Yiddish Proverb

When I was a boy of 14, my father was so ignorant, I could hardly stand to have the old man around. But when I got to be 21, I was astonished at how much the old man had learned in seven years.
    Mark Twain

A good father is one of the most unsung, unpraised, unnoticed, and yet one of the most valuable assets in our society.
    Billy Graham, American Evangelist

Fourth of July

On July 4, 1776, our forefathers signed the Declaration of Independence, and this is considered the birth of our nation. This manifesto, written by Thomas Jefferson with assistance from Ben Franklin and John Adams, is basically a listing of the bad things that the King of Great Britain was doing and a declaration that America is no longer tied to Great Britain. This was followed by the Constitution and the Bill of Rights to form a government that still stands today.

Declaration of Independence

Reading the Declaration of Independence is deeply educational. There are the oft-quoted words, like:

> [A]ll Men are created equal, that they are endowed by their Creator with certain unalienable Rights, that among these are Life, Liberty, and the Pursuit of Happiness.

Reading the entire document (see Appendix) is relatively easy, because it is only a few pages long—even our media-shortened attention spans can power through it. The introduction to the list is a bit more eloquent than "here's a list of bad things." It says:

> The History of the present King of Great-Britain is a History of repeated Injuries and Usurpations, all having in direct Object the Establishment of an absolute Tyranny over these States. To prove this, let Facts be submitted to a candid World.

This list is quite long, but interesting. You may say to yourself, "Wow, this list is familiar." Or you may say, "The more things change, the more they stay the same." Then you may wonder, "Where did these concepts of freedom and independence originate?" At the time, other governments were ruled by oppressive Kings and possibly some form of assemblies that were largely controlled by the Kings. You could go all the way back to Plato and Aristotle, or to the seventeenth-century philosopher John Locke, who observed that people are free by nature and that government exists to promote public good and protect life, liberty, and property. In 1689, Locke wrote the *Second Treatise on Government*, wherein he advocated governmental separation of powers and a government elected by society where the society holds the power to instate a new government when necessary.

In America, it was Thomas Paine who brought these ideas to the masses with his pamphlet *Common Sense*. With the Revolutionary War starting in April 1775, the American population was unsure whether to continue fighting or to reconcile with Great Britain. In January 1776, Thomas Paine wrote and published *Common Sense* to lay out the argument for continuing the revolution. This thirty-page booklet reviews the distinction between society and government, the perils of a monarchy and inherited power, a suggested organization for a new government, supporting arguments that America would win the war, and a call for a Declaration of Independence.

Paine's pamphlet went viral by today's standards. Over 500,000 copies were sold, and many more were copied. In addition, countless public readings occurred. *Common Sense* spoke to the ordinary citizen in a language they could understand. It was convincing in its presentation of the arguments for continuing the revolution. It is considered one of the most influential writings in history. A few quotes from *Common Sense* may be enough to get the point across:

> *Society is produced by our wants, and government by our wickedness; the former*

promotes our happiness positively by uniting our affections, the latter negatively by restraining our vices.

*

The king is not to be trusted without being looked after, or in other words, that a thirst for absolute power is the natural disease of monarchy.

*

[W]e see that bribery, corruption, and favoritism are the standing vices of kings.

*

For all men being originally equals, no one by birth could have a right to set up his own family in perpetual preference to all others forever.

*

Men who look upon themselves born to reign, and others to obey, soon grow insolent; selected from the rest of mankind, their minds are early poisoned by importance.

*

The nearer any government approaches to a republic the less business there is for a king.

*

If there is any true cause of fear respecting independence, it is because no plan is yet laid down. . . . I offer the following hints:

    Let the assemblies be annual, with a President only.

Let each colony be divided into . . . convenient districts, each district to send a proper number of delegates to Congress.

A committee of twenty-six members of Congress, viz. two for each colony.

*

The conferring members being met, let their business be to frame a Continental Charter . . . Securing freedom and property to all men, and above all things, the free exercise of religion, according to the dictates of conscience.

*

Every spot of the old world is overrun with oppression. Freedom had been hunted round the globe...O! receive the fugitive and prepare in time an asylum for mankind.

*

It is not in numbers, but in unity, that our great strength lies; yet our present numbers are sufficient to repel the force of all the world.

*

As to religion, I hold it to be the indispensable duty of all government to protect all conscientious professors thereof. . . . I fully and conscientiously believe that it is the will of the Almighty, that there should be diversity of religious opinions among us;

it affords a larger field for our Christian kindness.

*

To Conclude . . . nothing can settle our affairs so expeditiously as an open and determined declaration of independence. . . . Were a manifesto to be published, and dispatched to foreign courts, setting forth the miseries we have endured, and the peaceable methods we have ineffectually used for redress; declaring at the same time, that not being able, any longer, to live happily or safely under the cruel disposition of the British court, we had been driven to the necessity of breaking off all connections with her . . . such a memorial would produce more good effects to this Continent than if a ship were freighted with petitions to Britain.

*

So, there you have it. Thomas Jefferson, with John Adams and Ben Franklin, wrote the Declaration of Independence, but Thomas Paine told them how. You can see Mr. Paine was ahead of his time. Not only did he lay out the separation of powers, the House of Representative, and the Senate, he recognized that government by and for the people would be the envy of the world. He knew that we would become the wonderful melting pot that we are today. We just have to remember: "in unity, our great strength lies."

Constitution of the United States

Now you may be wondering, where is all that stuff about free speech?" Well, that is in the Bill of Rights, which are the first ten amendments to the Constitution of the United States. The First Amendment establishes free exercise of religion, freedom of speech, freedom of the press, freedom to assemble, and freedom to petition the government for a redress of grievances. All great things, right? The foundations of our democracy.

Our Founding Fathers defined these freedoms as freedoms from government intervention. For instance, before our independence, Great Britain prohibited American newspapers from publishing unfavorable articles. Uncensored and varied sources of information are critical to an informed democracy. These freedoms are the cornerstones of preserving our liberties. As such, any time a government official infringes upon these freedoms, it is a cause for concern as we grow from expressing humor, opinion, and facts through media outlets that range from the National Enquirer to newspapers and magazines, from cable and network news to Facebook and Twitter. Where do opinions end and the facts begin? Are government officials protecting the free press or attacking it? What would our Founding Fathers think today?

What about the Second Amendment and the right to bear arms? This was originally intended so that American citizens could form "a well-regulated militia" and protect themselves. Today things are a bit different with the firepower of available weapons. Simultaneously, the military capability of governments is beyond the imagination of many. Nonetheless, is the slightest infringement on the Second Amendment similar to the slightest infringements on the free press and the First Amendment? We all know "the pen is mightier than the sword" (Bulwer-Lytton, 1839), but we also know sometimes it is good to have a gun. Again, what would our Founding Fathers think today?

While our Founding Fathers were essentially rich men, and the constitution was written by and for themselves, they put everything at risk, and many gave up everything they had. They fought a war to make this happen, and many of them lost their homes, families, and lives to British soldiers. They meant what they said in the last line of the Declaration of Independence, "We mutually pledge to each other our lives, our fortunes, and our sacred honor."

Our Founding Fathers also recognized the need for change, and America has evolved. The Fourteenth Amendment granted black men the right to vote in 1870, and the Nineteenth Amendment granted women the right to vote in 1920. America continued to work toward eliminating voting barriers with the Twenty-fourth Amendment in 1964 prohibiting poll taxes, and the Civil Rights Voting Act in 1965, among other actions eliminating voting literacy tests. While great progress has been made, voting accessibility issues continue today.

Fourth of July is a time to reflect on how fortunate we are to live in such a great country with unparalleled personal freedoms. It was nearly 250 years ago that the Declaration of Independence was signed. The population was about 2.5 million, and life expectancy was about 35 years. Today, the population is more than 100 times larger, and life expectancy has doubled. Through all of this, our form of government has remained, and much of the free world has adopted its principles. Although much maligned, it seems easy to recognize that the alternatives could be much worse.

The American system of checks and balances has been grinding along slowly for centuries, and sometimes it appears that a few politicians want to stop it altogether. Whether it is being stopped by one branch or another is an open question. At the end of the day, however, outcomes will be decided by all of us, the voters.

Economic Freedom

We love this freedom to vote and "throw the bums out" when needed, although balance is essential. Freedom and balance in American business is similar: We can do what we want, as long as our customers and employees are happy. We have to charge a fair and competitive price, or else our customers will go elsewhere. We have to pay our employees in a similar fashion. Our customers need good products and our employees need good jobs. The markets keep us in balance, and that's a good thing.

Sometimes the markets get out of balance, even though the American economy is another envy of the world. How better to understand the economy than understanding the history of the greatest economic educational tool – Monopoly. Yes, the board game. It is very American, and its history is not well known.

Fourth of July

Credit is often given to Mr. Charles Darrow for inventing Monopoly, when it was actually Elizabeth Magie, a multi-talented woman from Maryland, who invented the famous game. Ms. Magie studied the teachings of economist Henry George who, in his book *Progress and Poverty* (1879), investigated the contradiction of wealth inequality and poverty during times of economic growth and technological progress.

Interestingly, more than 140 years ago people were discussing the distribution of wealth, when there was so much wealth to share due to technological progress. Ms. Magie wanted to demonstrate this with a board game that included land ownership. She created the game in 1903, and it was to be played two ways:

1. The players go around the board five times with all rents being paid to the center of the board. The players work together to spend the collected monies on new properties and improvements. The objective of the game

was to create as much wealth as possible for the players as a group.

2. The players go around the board an unlimited number of times with all rents being paid to the individual landowners. The game continues until one person has all of the money, and everyone else has gone bankrupt.

Ms. Magie thought that people would have more fun accumulating wealth together, and this would maximize enjoyment and serve as a demonstration for a better society. As we know, the winner-take-all version of the game proved to be more popular, even though bankruptcy in the real world is usually not much fun.

The game gained popularity across the Eastern states, and in 1933 Mr. Darrow improved the board by adding artwork, colors, and street names from Atlantic City, New Jersey, the most popular vacation town at the time. Mr. Darrow sold his version of the game to Parker Brothers, and the rest is history, including numerous patent battles. To date, over 275 million copies of the game have been sold in more than 111 countries around the world.

Today, real-world monopoly is alive and well in Atlantic City. The one-time elite vacation town suffered its own recession of sorts when inexpensive travel allowed other vacation spots, such as Florida and Las Vegas, to capture market share.

During the 1970s, Atlantic City welcomed large casinos to regain its status as an elite vacation destination. Unfortunately, a number of casinos made money during the good times, and then filed bankruptcy during the bad times. Today, Atlantic City continues to regain its prominence as a vacation destination.

Unlike the board game, bankruptcy in America is not always the end of the game. We have bankruptcy laws to protect the unfortunate. No debtor's prisons exist in America, and we can be proud of our resilience and perseverance while entrepreneurship thrives in America.

Proud to be American

The Fourth of July is also a time to ask, "What makes you proud to be an American?" Everyone has a different answer. Of course, there are similar answers, but each is unique in its meaning and in the individual's source of inspiration. Freedom and liberty are dominant themes, and so are equality, inclusion, and caring.

America is unique because we are not a nation formed and held together by ancestry or race. We are held together by beliefs. As a democracy, our

unified values provide our foundation, and our informed participation provides continuous improvement. It's not a perfect system, but it's much better than the next-best alternative. We are the great experiment, and these shared values are the universal reason we are all proud to be Americans.

Quotes to Ponder

We have it in our power to begin the world over again.
      Thomas Paine

Those who give up freedom in order to gain security will not have, nor do they deserve to have, either one.
      Benjamin Franklin

Fourth of July

I like to see a man proud of the place in which he lives. I like to see a man live so that his place will be proud of him.
    Abraham Lincoln

Sometimes people call me an idealist. Well, that is the way I know I am an American. America is the only idealistic nation in the world.
    Woodrow Wilson

Labor Day

Labor Day says goodbye to summer and hello to fall. The return of school brings about a sense of a fresh start and renewed resolutions. The same applies to work and career as the seasons change, and Labor Day should remind us of past struggles that have made our careers possible.

Labor Day is interesting because it celebrates everyday life—most of us have a job where labor laws are applied. Most of us must work for a living, and we search for that combination of enjoyable work, equitable pay, and societal benefit or the deeper meaning that makes everything worthwhile—that "labor of love."

One thing to remember from high school is that history tells the story of the haves vs. the have-nots. Labor history reflects this. Labor protests were frequent and often violent dating back to the

1600s and intensifying through the 1800s across numerous industries, from agriculture to textiles and nearly everything in between.

Labor Day originated with the Knights of Labor and other labor organizations holding an assembly and parade in support of the laboring classes in New York City, on September 5, 1882. Labor unions, however, were first organized in the early 1800s and grew in numbers and effectiveness throughout that century. The Knights of Labor became one of the largest, if not the first, nationwide labor union. In 1884, the American Federation of Organized Trades and Labor Unions declared that by May 1, 1886, the eight-hour workday would be in effect across the United

States. When legislators and employers failed to comply by that time, the parade became a demonstration in Chicago.

By May 4, police and protesters engaged in a deadly confrontation at Chicago's Haymarket Square. Police shot protesters, and a bomb exploded within the crowd. Overall, eleven people were killed, including seven police officers, while many more were injured. Eight suspects were arrested and convicted on limited information: four were executed, one committed suicide in his cell, and three were pardoned in 1893. Governor Altgeld of Illinois proclaimed at the time of the pardon:

> The deed to sentencing the Haymarket men was wrong, a miscarriage of justice. And the truth is that the great multitudes annually arrested are poor, the unfortunate, the young, and the neglected. In short, our penal machinery seems to recruit its victims from among those who are fighting an unequal fight in the struggle for existence.

Oregon was the first state to have a Labor Day holiday, in 1887, although it did not become a national holiday until 1894, after the Pullman Strike.

In Pullman, Illinois, the Pullman Company reduced wages and nearly 4,000 workers began a strike that grew into a nation-wide railroad strike that lasted from May into July of 1894. An estimated 250,000 workers in 27 states participated in the strike. Clashes between railroad agents, federal troops, and strikers resulted in 30 strikers being killed, 57 wounded, and over $80 million in property damage.

After President Cleveland ordered federal suppression of the Pullman Strike, he had to gain favor with the labor movement. There was great concern that the May 1 holiday would encourage annual violence in commemoration of the Haymarket Riot, so President Cleveland joined several states and made the first Monday in September Labor Day—a federal holiday in honor of the working person. Cleveland's political tactic, however, didn't achieve its desired effect. Cleveland lost the Democratic Party's 1896 nomination to William Jennings Bryan (who lost the presidential election to William McKinley).

Establishing Labor Day in 1894 was just a marker of labor struggles building throughout the Industrial Revolution of the American economy. Company towns and labor camps existed under deplorable conditions. Take the coal mining industry as one example where generations of miners and families were paid in company script, to be spent at the company stores, while their children went to company schools. Working conditions were extremely dangerous, with on-the-job fatalities and black-lung disease. Living conditions were not much better under extreme poverty, inadequate shelter, and limited pay to buy food. The workers began organizing in the early 1900s and staged one of their first strikes in the Paint Creek-Cabin Creek strike of 1912. This bloody encounter did not improve working conditions, nor did it deter the resolve of miners to improve their working and living conditions. In 1921, armed miner workers entered into a full-on militarized battle with armed private security forces hired by the mining companies in the Battle of Blair Mountain. Federal troops were finally called in by President Harding to defeat the miners. The union miners were later charged with treason and murder. They were acquitted and eventually went back to work, and the labor movement continued.

Labor History from Slavery to Labor Laws

Labor history, however, begins with slaves and indentured servants. Although black slaves were first brought to the Colony of Virginia in 1619, it was the Virginia Governor's Council decision in 1640 when the first legal racial distinction was recorded. In this case, a black runaway indentured servant was sentenced to a lifetime of servitude, while his white indentured servant cohorts were sentenced to only a few additional years of servitude. When it comes to slavery and racism in America, here is a short list of realities that are important to remember today:

1. Race differences are man-made. Put a group of toddlers together and they are all friends. The racial differences are socially constructed.

2. People developed and promoted white supremacy to justify slavery, and the results of those social constructions are woven throughout our society.

3. America's current racism is largely due to a lack of understanding of the legacy issues of slavery that are still with us today.

4. America, at its best, represents the integration of all races and all individuals.

5. Integration is a slow, never-ending process.

Our government moves too slowly and often contrarily to our preferred direction. Take child labor, for instance. Organized movements to limit child labor were initiated in 1904, but it took these groups twelve years to persuade Congress to pass a law in 1916. This law, however, was struck down by the Supreme Court, and the children were "allowed" to go back to work. It wasn't until the Great Depression, when there were not enough jobs for the adults, that child labor laws were enacted in 1938 to limit the labor force. That's 34 years that it took to agree that kids should stay in school instead of working in factories.

Today we take for granted the eight-hour workday, the forty-hour workweek, child labor laws, and other worker protections. It's hard to imagine that riots occurred and lives were lost to achieve these laws, while today we consider health care and retirement benefits for all workers a standard practice. How will this affect work in today's global world, as American capital migrates to economic efficiencies (i.e., cheap labor) around the world?

> *Most people come to work every day and want to do a good job. Poor definition and poor motivation just get in the way.*
> Anonymous

Sometimes you're lucky to have a good job. Sometimes you're lucky to hire good people.
    Robert Payan

With a career, there is not enough time in the day. . . . With a job, there is too much time in the day.
    Chris Rock

We know that work is essential, but today it is balanced by limited work hours, worker protections, and benefits. At the same time, the pendulum swings. Government regulations become too complex to understand, unions become corrupt and too powerful, benefits grow to be unaffordable, and people abuse the systems designed to protect them. What unfair employers and disgruntled employees fail to recognize is that finding happiness in your work is one of the keys to long-term happiness in life.

Happiness is the pursuit of a worthy goal.
    Earl Nightingale

Sports Labor

The three-day Labor Day weekend that celebrates workers' rights also coincides with the baseball season nearing another conclusion and the NFL kicking off a new season. Hopefully, all these overpriced athletes realize that they owe it all to Curt Flood.

Curt Flood was an all-star center fielder for the St. Louis Cardinals who was traded to the Philadelphia Phillies after the 1969 season. Curt, however, decided that he didn't want to move to Philadelphia and refused. He sat out the 1970 season and endured a lengthy trial that eventually went to the Supreme Court in 1972. Curt lost the battle, and he only played professional baseball for a few more months. But he won the war. In 1976, free agency became a reality, and today professional athletes are being paid fair market value.

To put it into perspective, in 1969 as an all-star center fielder, Curt Flood made $90,000 per year. That's not bad—in today's dollars that would be about $600,000. Now, however, the minimum wage for a major league baseball player is $560,000, the average salary is $4,400,000, and the largely unknown center fielder for the Los Angeles Angels makes $36,000,000 per year.

We've come a long way since the first Labor Day. In addition to the history given above, we currently also have a mind-boggling system of laws and regulations governing nearly every aspect of hiring someone—all to help achieve worthy goals. It's mostly all good. Business has learned that working a person 80 hours a week for little pay leaves no one to purchase the products. OSHA has taught us that safe work practices actually prevent injuries and fatalities and promote a healthier workforce. Diversity in the workplace has taught us that we are all in this together.

The next time you celebrate Labor Day, remember to stay motivated and enjoy your work; each of us is fortunate to be wherever we are. Recognize that any task is a piece of a larger goal that includes not only the task, but also our own personal growth. In addition, be aware that when Americans work for a fair wage and deliver a quality product, Americans should also be able to afford to purchase the products of their labor. Here's to knowing that a successful American economy is here for the owners, the workers, and even for those in need.

Quotes to Ponder

Pleasure in the job puts perfection in the work.
　　　　　　　　Aristotle

The best way to find yourself is to lose yourself in the service of others.
　　　　　　　Mahatma Gandhi

Labor Day

Our merchants and masters complain much of the bad effects of high wages in raising the price and lessening the sale of goods. They say nothing concerning the bad effects of high profits. They are silent with regard to the pernicious effects of their own gains. They complain only of those of other people.
  Adam Smith, *An Inquiry into the Nature
  and Causes of the Wealth of Nations*

History is a great teacher. Now, everyone knows that the labor movement did not diminish the strength of the nation but enlarged it. By raising the living standards of millions, labor miraculously created a market for industry.
        Martin Luther King Jr.

Columbus Day / Indigenous Peoples' Day

In 1492, Christopher Columbus sailed the ocean blue in the *Nina*, the *Pinta*, and the *Santa Maria*. This is what most Americans remember from elementary school about Columbus discovering America, but there is more to the story, much more.

First of all, Columbus did not land his ships in America. He landed in the Bahamas and never set foot on what is now the United States. Second of all, there were already people in the Bahamas and America. Was it really a discovery?

Columbus was an Italian-born explorer who was commissioned by Spain to travel west and sail around the globe to Asia and India. When Columbus landed, he thought he was in India. In a manner of speaking, maybe he discovered America for those in southern Europe who did

not know that America existed or that the Atlantic and Pacific were two separate oceans.

As far as European discoveries go, the Vikings in northern Europe "discovered" North America nearly 500 years earlier, when Viking ships landed in Newfoundland. There is also substantial evidence that the Americas were populated by migration from Asia over 12,000 years ago, and some historians recognize that Chinese explorers discovered the western shores of America in the early 1400s. There is no doubt, however, that Columbus paved the way for European exploration and eventual colonization of the Americas that led to the birth of our nation.

Columbus Day/Indigenous Peoples' Day

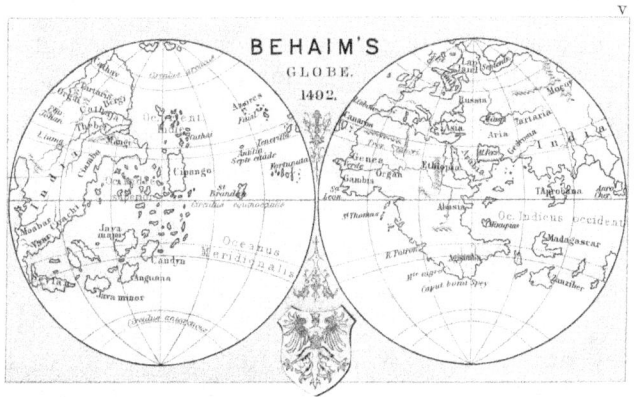

Columbus Day celebrations in the United States began in 1792, on the 300th anniversary of Columbus's landing, organized by Tammany Hall, a political organization formed in New York City during the late 1700s. As a political organization, it originally sought to help the poor and immigrant populations, but later developed a reputation for corruption. Its power ebbed and flowed over the years and eventually dissolved in the 1960s.

Many Italian and Catholic communities felt proud of Columbus's heritage and began annual celebrations including parades and religious ceremonies. In 1892, President Benjamin Harrison issued a proclamation for Americans to celebrate the 400th anniversary of Columbus's discovery with patriotic festivities.

The Knights of Columbus, another religious/social/political organization, lobbied Congress and the White House. In 1937 President Roosevelt made October 12 Columbus Day, a national holiday. Columbus Day was changed to the second Monday in October as part of the National Holiday Act of 1971.

The reality of Christopher Columbus's discovery may not be worthy of his hero status and the patriotic celebration that the holiday intends. Columbus was not necessarily in search of new lands as much as he was searching for new conquests. When Columbus arrived in the Bahamas, he took ownership of the land and enslaved the natives. He called the natives "Indians," although they were not in India as Columbus thought, and he forced them into labor under brutal circumstances to mine for riches and work the plantations. Many natives were taken back to Spain to be sold as slaves. In addition, Columbus and his men unintentionally introduced new diseases that killed many of the natives.

The behavior of Christopher Columbus may have been common for his day, and maybe it is unfair to apply today's standards to people of a different place and time. On the other hand, should we celebrate these conquests as noble and with high regard?

Columbus Day/Indigenous Peoples' Day

It turns out that Columbus was not much different than the European settlers that followed, such as when the *Mayflower* landed on Plymouth Rock in 1620. Taking lands forcibly from the Native Americans and building a thriving economy on the backs of poor-white and slave labor are tragic realities of our history. These realities cannot be changed. The question is, can they be overcome?

There is a growing movement in the United States to recognize Native Americans and other indigenous peoples instead of Christopher Columbus. In fact, numerous states and countless cities have replaced Columbus Day with Indigenous Peoples' Day. This movement may continue to grow as greater awareness is given to the sufferings and

contributions of the indigenous populations throughout the Americas when European explorers arrived and imposed their new rules, religions, and cultures across the land.

Quotes to Ponder

Here are a few quotes to ponder as we consider the true meaning of Columbus Day.

> *You can never cross the ocean unless you have the courage to lose sight of the shore.*
> Christopher Columbus

> *If Columbus had an advisory committee, he would probably still be at the dock.*
> Arthur Goldberg, former Associate Justice of the US Supreme Court

> *In 1492, the natives discovered they were Indians, discovered they lived in America, discovered they were naked, discovered that the Sin existed, discovered they owed allegiance to a King and Kingdom from another world and a God from another sky.*
> Eduardo Galeano, author,
> Los Hijos de los Días (Children of the Days: A Calendar of Human History)

Columbus Day/Indigenous Peoples' Day

The first peace, which is the most important, is that which comes within the souls of people when they realize their relationship, their oneness, with the universe and all its powers, and when they realize that at the center of the universe dwells Wakan-Tanka [the Great Spirit], and that this center is really everywhere, it is within each of us. This is the real peace, and the others are but reflections of this. The second peace is that which is made between two individuals, and the third is that which is made between two nations. But above all you should understand that there can never be peace between nations until there is known that true peace, which, as I have often said, is within the souls of men.

      Black Elk, Wichasha Wakan
      [Holy Man] of the Oglala Lakota

Halloween

Halloween originated 2,000 years ago with the ancient Celtic festival of Samhain, in the areas of Ireland, England, and northern France. The Celts celebrated the new year on November 1, with the passing of summer into the cold darkness of winter. On the night before the new year, the Celts believed the boundary between the worlds of the living and the dead became blurred. It was believed that on this night the ghosts of the dead returned to the earth, and this made it easier for the Celtic religious leaders to make predictions for the upcoming year.

Sacred bonfires were built, and people gathered to burn crops and offer animal sacrifices to the Celtic gods. The Celts wore costumes and had their fortunes told. Rituals honoring the dead were practiced, such as placing a candle by an open window to guide the departed back home. When the Samhain celebrations were over, people re-lit their hearth fires with coals from the sacred bonfires, to help protect them during the coming winter.

By 43 CE, the Roman Empire conquered most of the Celtic territory, and the ancient traditions were combined with those of the Catholic Church. Around 700 CE, Pope Gregory III created All Saints Day to be observed on November 1, also called All-Hallows Day from a Middle English translation of All-Saints. The traditional nighttime celebrations became All-Hallows Eve, and eventually Halloween.

Halloween was limited in colonial New England by the Protestant belief systems, although it was popular in the southern American colonies. As new immigrants flooded to America, including millions of Irish fleeing Ireland's potato famine of 1846, Halloween became a popular celebration on a national scale.

In the late 1800s Americans molded Halloween into a holiday of community and neighborly parties. Ghosts, pranks, and witchcraft were eliminated, and the focus was on games, foods of the season, and costumes. Encouraged by newspapers and community leaders, the frightening,

superstitious, and religious overtones were lost. Between the 1920s and 1950s, the age-old tradition of trick-or-treating was revived, and families could prevent a trick (or prank) by giving a treat.

The passing of summer to winter was a scary time back in the day when the chance of death loomed large over the long, cold winters. Some may interpret the earliest ceremonies of Halloween as a satanic holiday that included worshiping bad ghosts and other horrible things. At the same time, a person may wonder, "Should I be afraid of ghosts?"

Nowadays, ghosts visit us frequently through television and movies. Some are "good" and delightful, like Casper the Friendly Ghost. In the movie *Ghost*, Patrick Swayze was a good ghost and Demi Moore was lucky he came back to save her. In *Field of Dreams*, those ghosts just wanted to play baseball. *Beetlejuice*, *Ghost Town*, and *Ghost Dad* all depicted good ghosts—but that's about it. Most all other ghosts in the movies are scary creatures, and some inspire great costumes.

Americans spend $6 billion annually on Halloween, making it one of the larger commercial holidays. From neighborhood block parties to handing out candy on the doorstep, Halloween carries on the most ancient of traditions that bring family and friends together to welcome the darkness of winter with the blessings of gods and spirits. Although brought to the United States from northern Europe and expanded by immigration after the Irish potato famine, it is truly an American holiday in the spirit of community and friendship. Here's to wishing that all your ghosts are friendly ghosts, on Halloween and throughout the year.

Halloween

Quotes to Ponder

The truth is that monsters are real, and ghosts are real, too. They live inside us, and sometimes they win.
    Stephen King

Count me in for any holiday that includes dressing in costumes, role playing, and candy.
    Anonymous

If a man harbors any sort of fear, it makes him a landlord to a ghost.
    Lloyd Douglas, minister and American author

Veterans Day

It has been more than 100 years since the end of World War I—and the beginnings of our Veterans Day celebrations.

In the early 1900s, European countries strengthened their military capabilities and formed strategic alliances with commitments to assist and defend each other. At the same time, imperialism was common, as many countries tried to expand their empires through acquisition, exchange, and conquest of colonies. The colonies' aspirations, however, were rarely in alignment with the imperialistic desires of the larger countries.

Increased military preparedness, strategic alliances, imperialism, and nationalism were the dominoes in place when Archduke Ferdinand of Austria-Hungary was assassinated by a Serbian nationalist on June 28, 1914. Austria-Hungary shortly thereafter declared war on Serbia, Russia came to Serbia's defense, and Germany came to Hungary-Austria's defense. France and Great Britain were Russian allies, and WW I was in full swing.

The United States tried to stay out of the war, but we had merchant ships doing business in Great Britain, and a few of these ships were sunk by German U-boats. There were German atrocities of war that infuriated the United States, and Germany tried to encourage Mexico to attack the US. Some historians will say the real reason the US joined the war was Wall Street. J. P. Morgan and friends had $3 billion in loans to France and Great Britain and could not afford a German victory. They lobbied President Wilson to join the war or run the risk of bankrupting the US economy (too big to fail). Whether it was German atrocities and changing American sentiment, financial considerations, or German attacks on US ocean liners, the result was the same. The US entered the war in 1917, and the Great War ended with the signing of an armistice on November 11, 1918, and the Treaty of Versailles on June 28, 1919.

In less than five years of war, approximately 17 million people died in WW I, and an estimated 20 million people were wounded. The US sent 2 million well-equipped troops to Europe, and 100,000 US soldiers died. At the same time, the 1918 Spanish Flu (H1N1 influenza virus) pandemic killed over 50 million people worldwide.

WW I was a brutal war with significant suffering and tragedy beyond the battlefields. Prior to 1914, war was considered noble and glorious. After 1918, it was something that should never happen again. It became known as the war to end all wars.

President Wilson first commemorated Armistice Day in 1919, and it became a legal holiday in 1926. Armistice Day was set aside to honor the veterans of WW I and was dedicated to the cause of world peace. In 1954, after WW II and the Korean War, the holiday was changed in the United States to Veterans Day, to honor veterans of all American conflicts. The Uniform Holiday Bill of 1968 changed the date to late October for convenience, but the historic and patriotic significance of the 11th day in the 11th month was overwhelming, and the date was changed back to November 11 in 1974.

Veterans Day leaves us plenty to ponder each year as we honor our veterans and celebrate our commitment to continued peace among nations. This truly is the holiday that celebrates the phrase "those who don't know history are condemned to repeat it." As arms races come and go, WW I taught us that military might leads to over-confidence and the propensity to initiate military conflicts. This is also balanced by Teddy Rosevelt's proclamation, "Walk softly and carry a big stick." There are no easy answers as our leaders strive for mutual economic prosperity and peaceful coexistence.

We can be proud as Americans to be the leaders of peace and prosperity. By skill and good fortune, America emerged from the World Wars as the example of economic and military power created through a society of individual freedom, self-rule, and social equality. While we are not perfect, these lofty goals are the aspirations of most people worldwide.

Veterans' Day

Quotes to Ponder

Armistice Day will be filled with solemn pride in the heroism of those who died in the country's service and with gratitude for the victory, both because of the thing from which it has freed us and because of the opportunity it has given America to show her sympathy with peace and justice in the councils of the nations.
   President Woodrow Wilson, 1919

Armistice Day . . . thanksgiving and prayer and exercises designed to perpetuate peace through goodwill and mutual understanding between nations.
   US Congress, 1926

We must concentrate not merely on the negative expulsion of war, but on the positive affirmation of peace.
   Martin Luther King, Jr.

Peace is not the absence of conflict; it is the ability to handle conflict by peaceful means.
   Ronald Reagan

Thanksgiving

Most Americans have been taught that Thanksgiving began in 1621 when the Native Americans assisted the Pilgrims with growing corn and other essentials of life in their New World. As we recall from third grade, the Pilgrims were so grateful that they invited the Native Americans to a feast as an expression of their gratitude.

This one-time Pilgrim/Native American event may, or may not, have occurred—and autumn harvest festivals remained common in some of the colonies—but it did not establish the Thanksgiving holiday. In fact, it was 200 years later that Ms. Sarah Josepha Hale created the Thanksgiving that we celebrate today.

During the American Revolution, the Continental Congress declared several days of thanksgiving following military victories. George Washington, with John Adams and James Madison, issued a proclamation to observe a national day of thanks to celebrate the end of the Revolutionary War and establishment of the US Constitution. Thomas Jefferson opposed the holiday because he thought it crossed the line between church and state.

Sarah Josepha Hale was a remarkable writer, editor, and publisher in the 1800s. She authored "Mary Had a Little Lamb" and also founded the *American Ladies Magazine*. Later she was the editor of *Godey's Lady Book*. For over 40 years, Ms. Hale was the equivalent of a modern-day Martha Stewart or Oprah Winfrey through the most widely distributed magazine covering issues from women's rights to housekeeping.

Ms. Hale began lobbying legislators in the 1840s to establish a national thanksgiving holiday. Her efforts included writing to five different presidents over the years. Eventually 30 states celebrated a form of Thanksgiving, but Ms. Hale wanted a national holiday to unify Americans across the north-south political divide.

Christmas

During the Civil War, Confederate President Jefferson Davis declared days of thanksgiving following victories in 1861 and 1862. President Lincoln followed with similar declarations following victories by the North in 1862 and 1863. Ms. Hale wrote President Lincoln in September 1863, and within a week he declared Thanksgiving Day a national holiday to be observed on the 4th Thursday in November.

Thanksgiving has turned into an American favorite. It brings us together as a nation with shared joys and gratitude. It is a day like no other. It has become uniquely patriotic, with traditions of family, friends, food, and football.

Football? Actually, Thanksgiving Day came first in 1863, but the American Intercollegiate Football Association held its first championship game on Thanksgiving Day in 1876. High school and college football games quickly caught on, and the tradition grew to more than 5,000 games taking place on Thanksgiving Day by the 1890s. The NFL took over the tradition when the Detroit Lions played the Chicago Bears in 1934. The Lions have played every year on Thanksgiving Day since then, except during the World War II years from 1939 to 1944. Some of your family traditions may date back to that first NFL football game during the Great Depression.

Food in America

One of the primary ways we celebrate Thanksgiving is with food. In her 1827 novel, *Northwood: Life North and South*, the impressive Sarah Josepha Hale devoted an entire chapter to a day of thanksgiving. She solidified many of the traditions and recipes that we enjoy today.

Even in times of food shortages, Thanksgiving abundance has been honored. In 1934, during the Great Depression, a Thanksgiving meal for four cost nearly 20 percent of the average household monthly income—more than the monthly rent. The meal also required significant labor to complete without the aid of many canned, frozen, or otherwise conveniently packaged ingredients that we enjoy today.

Land Grant Colleges

Yes, we celebrate Thanksgiving with food, while our access to food has increased tremendously over the past couple of centuries. During the Civil War, the Land Grant College Act of 1862 shored up the nation's future in agriculture. The Act granted federal land to states to create colleges that specialized in agriculture and mechanics. This Act also provided federal land that states could sell to farmers to help pay for the colleges. The Act was a monumental success, initially throughout the non-Confederate states, with schools such as Kansas State, Michigan State, University of California at Berkeley, Cornell University, and the Massachusetts Institute of Technology (MIT). The program was expanded throughout the country in 1890, and today there are 75 Land Grant universities and 31 Native American tribal colleges. One of the earliest and most prestigious graduates was George Washington Carver.

George Washington Carver was born a slave in 1864 in Diamond, Missouri. His family was stolen by slave raiders when George was an infant. George and his brother were recovered by his original owner, but not his mother and sister. As a small and often sickly child, George tended to household chores and was taught to read and write by the women of the house. He left home at age eleven, to pursue education. George bounced around Missouri and Kansas, ultimately graduating from high school. He next found his way to the first land grant college, Iowa State, to study agriculture. Mr. Carver graduated with a Bachelor of Science degree in 1894, and a Master of Science in 1896.

Mr. Carver became a professor at Tuskegee University, a land grant college in Alabama, where he pioneered crop rotation science during a period when most Southern farmers believed they didn't need any help from educated college types. The farmers, however, were so impressed with Carver's methods of rotating between cotton, peanuts, sweet potatoes, and soybeans that he quickly became an agricultural legend. With the overabundance of crop production, Carver

developed alternative uses for these food crops, such as oils, flours, cosmetics, stains, dyes, inks, and soaps, to name a few. Carver spent the rest of his life at Tuskegee and, following his death in 1943, President Franklin Delano Roosevelt established a national monument at Carver's childhood home—the first non-president to have a national monument in their honor.

Water Supply

America further developed our food production capabilities by "reclaiming" farmland from the arid deserts in the Southwest. First passed in 1902, the Reclamation Act eventually established the Bureau of Reclamation that led to the creation of vast water storage and irrigation capacities in 17 western states. The early going was difficult, given the expectation that the farmers would be able to repay the infrastructure investment. This did not develop, and the repayment plans were modified to longer repayment terms, to payments based on "ability to pay," and finally debt forgiveness. Reclamation's first significant success was the Boulder Canyon (Hoover) Dam on the Colorado River in 1928. The infusion of federal funding helped ease some of the dust bowl hardship and economic depression of the 1930s, but the program truly thrived after World War II. From the 1930s through the 1960s, the

Bureau of Reclamation designed and constructed thousands of water supply facilities, including Hoover Dam, Shasta Dam, Grand Coulee Dam, and Glenn Canyon Dam—each the tallest dams of their kind when constructed. Today, the Bureau operates and maintains 338 reservoirs, 492 dams, 8,000 miles of irrigation canals, and supplies water to 30 million people in 17 western states. This federal investment in infrastructure also provides irrigation water to 140,000 farmers and over 10,000,000 acres of farmland. In addition, the Bureau operates 53 hydroelectric power plants generating over 40 billion kilowatt-hours of electricity each year, enough for over 3.5 million households.

Electricity

Getting electricity was another major obstacle for rural America and, in turn, food production. During the 1930s, only 3 percent of rural homes had electricity. It was not economical to provide long-distance power distribution for a few homes throughout rural areas, and therefore, farmers were left in the dark.

The Rural Electrification Act of 1936 provided federal loans, engineering, and crews to install electrical distribution lines, and home and farm wiring systems. This infusion of federal investment following WW II provided electrical power to over 90 percent of farm homes by 1959.

The investments in science from seeds and soils to machinery, to irrigation water and electricity, increased crop production dramatically. The interstate highway system was started in the late 1950s as a defense readiness system, but also allowed for the transport of food supplies and products across great distances. Product markets were also developed by the 1946 National School Lunch program, and nutrition education saw advancement. The 1947 General Agreement on Tariffs and Trade, as well as the 1954 Agricultural Trade Development and Assistance Act, facilitated agricultural exports and foreign aid.

Cold War / Food War

As we think about post-WW II food, consider also the Cold War with Russia. The Cold War was a war of prosperity that had to be won to validate and preserve our political and economic systems—a food war of sorts. At the same time, the United States was eager to share our knowledge of crop production and utilization. Russian leader Nikita Khrushchev visited Iowa farms in 1959. It is interesting that the science and technologies of the American farm did not translate to the Russian economic system, and Khrushchev was

© The Des Moines Register – USA TODAY NETWORK

"Now there's a real American!" Nikita Khrushchev says as he pats Iowan Jack Christensen's belly.

largely ineffective in transforming food production capabilities in Russia. The social democracy of American government investment and capitalized agriculture production was successful, while the authoritarian form of communism resulted in food shortages, rationing, and bread lines.

The vast American food industry, however, does come with costs. The business of supply and demand has not provided the greatest nutritional model. Some contend that ignoring the conclusions of the McGovern nutritional study in the early 1970s and placing an emphasis on processed foods has created an obese society with expensive health issues. The environment has also suffered. Climate change is altering water supplies and ecosystems are being lost. At the same time, once these problems are recognized and addressed, there is little doubt that the American way will find and implement solutions.

Gratitude

Today, spices and recipes from around the world influence Thanksgiving such that the meal has become an affordable culinary adventure, from pumpkin soups, eccentric appetizers, fine wines, and outrageous side dishes, to dozens of variations on the traditional turkey. We owe so much to the scientists, engineers, farmers, builders, producers, and distributors that allow us to grow enough food to feed 300 million people every day in the United States and still export enough to feed a large portion of the world.

Gratitude is overflowing on Thanksgiving, although it continues unnoticed throughout much of the year. The simple pleasures in life, like a hot shower and a warm bed, are overlooked every day, and our empathy for those without gets lost.

Thanksgiving provides an opportunity to remember how fortunate we are.

Gratitude also gets lost in the daily struggles of good and evil. Whether it is work, health, finances, or other struggles, Thanksgiving gives us an opportunity to realize that Evil is the illusion, and Good will prevail. Just like in the movies, it is often true in real life as well. It may seem like Mufasa has died and Scar has taken over the Pride Lands, but give things time, and eventually Simba will arrive and save the day.

Now there's a good idea—add *The Lion King* to the Thanksgiving Day tradition. A great family movie. At the end of the day, watch a good movie, eat dessert, lick the plate, and be forever grateful.

Here's to a wonderful Thanksgiving holiday, full of rich traditions. As we pay homage to Sarah Josepha Hale and the agricultural industry, we are all so fortunate to enjoy the family, friends, and food that surround us every day.

Quotes to Ponder

With great gratitude and patriotism on Thanksgiving Day, here are a few quotes to ponder:

Thanksgiving

Nor need we power or splendor, wide hall or lordly dome

The good, the true, the tender—these form the wealth of home.
Sarah Josepha Hale

Small cheer and great welcome make a merry feast.
William Shakespeare

He is a wise man who does not grieve for the things which he has not, but rejoices for those which he has.
Epictetus, 1st-century Greek philosopher

Democracy cannot succeed unless those who express their choice are prepared to choose wisely. The real safeguard of democracy, therefore, is education.
Franklin D. Roosevelt

Be thankful for what you have; you'll end up having more. If you concentrate on what you don't have, you will never, ever have enough.
Oprah Winfrey

When I started counting my blessings, my whole life turned around.
Willie Nelson

At times, our own light goes out and is rekindled by a spark from another person. Each of us has cause to think with deep gratitude of those who have lighted the flame within us.
Albert Schweitzer

Christmas

Christmas is the sacred, worldwide Christian holiday and cultural phenomenon to celebrate the birth of Jesus Christ, Son of God. From the biblical account of Joseph and Mary looking for a place to spend the night and Jesus's birth in a manger in the town of Bethlehem, to the three wise men bringing gifts of gold, frankincense, and myrrh, this religious holiday celebrates God's own child and gift to mankind. Christians hold that, through faith in Jesus Christ, every person can be saved and can live an eternal life in heaven.

> *For unto you is born this day in the City of David a savior, which is Christ the Lord. And this shall be a sign unto you; Ye shall find the babe wrapped in swaddling clothes, lying in a manger.*
> Luke 02:08-14

Christmas also has roots in an ancient holiday dating before the birth of Jesus Christ. Early pagan celebrations recognized the winter solstice as the return of the sun. In Rome, Saturn was the god of agriculture and Saturnalia became the ancient Roman midwinter holiday. Saturnalia would begin in mid-December and continue through the winter solstice. Pine boughs and fir trees were used as decorations to spark remembrance that spring would return from the darkness of winter. The Romans would stop working and celebrate with music, food, social activities, and gift giving. Candles, signifying light after the solstice, were common gifts. Saturnalia was a drunken, riotous holiday, similar to Mardi Gras of today, with chaos taking the place of normal Roman order.

In the fourth century CE, the church began celebrating the birth of Jesus as a holiday. The Bible does not define the date, while herding shepherds suggest it may have been in the spring or summer. Nonetheless, Pope Julius I chose December 25 as the day, likely to coincide with the celebrations of Saturnalia, thereby helping to increase Christianity's acceptance and popularity. Or maybe Pope Julius I thought it might be a good idea to bring the light of Jesus Christ to mankind during the darkest time of the year.

Throughout the Middle Ages (5th through 12th centuries CE), Christianity replaced most of the pagan celebrations, and Christmas became a time to attend church before participating in the more wild and disorderly activities. Conversely, in the 17th century, Christmas was cancelled in England by Puritan Oliver Cromwell, who wanted to eliminate decadence.

Cromwell was an English military leader who took control of England, Wales, Scotland, and Ireland after the execution of King Charles I. As "Lord Protector," Cromwell ruled from 1653 to 1658, using his military strength to maintain power and impose a godly rule rather than rule by the people. Blasphemy, cursing, drunkenness, and adultery were outlawed. Following Cromwell's death, Charles II returned to England and restored the monarchy.

In America, the pilgrims arriving in 1620 were also orthodox Puritans, similar to Cromwell. In fact, Christmas was outlawed in Boston from 1659 to 1681. English customs, including Christmas, fell out of favor through the American Revolution and beyond. It was not until the early 1800s that America reinvented Christmas celebrations.

Author Washington Irving wrote a series of stories in the early 1800s depicting a Christmas setting where the wealthy invited peasants into their homes to celebrate a peaceful, heart-warming holiday. Some may say that Irving's stories invented the Christmas traditions that we celebrate today. In 1822, with "'Twas the Night Before Christmas," by the Episcopal minister Clement Clarke Moore, that the current version of Santa Claus was established. In 1843, English author Charles Dickens published *A Christmas Carol* and furthered the traditions of family, kindness, and generosity during Christmas. On June 28, 1870, Christmas was declared a federal holiday, along with New Year's Day, Independence Day, and Thanksgiving Day, under the first federal holiday law.

The traditions of Christmas are more of an American creation from the 1800s, when the nation was growing in many different directions, than they are ageless religious ceremonies. In one direction, the infant economy was developing, western expansion was exploding, and immigrants fueled a population seeking economic opportunity and spiritual freedom. In another direction, financial systems were being created to the advantage of some and disadvantage of others. The separation of economic classes was a problem. The Civil War separated the nation further, and Reconstruction was tasked with bringing together friends, families, and races. Some may say that Americans built the traditions of Christmas around the birth and teachings of Jesus Christ without realizing that we were solving the enormous cultural problems of the times. Today, Christmas trees, holiday

cards, shared meals, lights, and Santa Claus are as much American as they are ancient traditions.

Santa Claus dates back to the third century near Myra, Turkey, where Saint Nicholas was known for his kindness, charity, and protection of children. Today, children believe that Santa flies through the skies and delivers presents. As they grow older, children wonder if Santa Claus is real. The answer is a resounding YES. Observant teenagers wonder if Santa Claus is a gimmick and a sham designed to commercialize the holiday season. Not so.

Sure, Santa Claus is not flesh and bones, living at the North Pole. Rather, Santa Claus is the feeling you get when you see something and know that it is the perfect gift for someone else. You then give the gift to that special person because it makes you feel good inside. That feeling inside is Santa Claus. So, be joyous no matter what the gift is that you give or receive. Whether it is last year's calendar because someone thinks you will like the pictures or a can of tuna because they know you are on a high-protein diet, it's all good. It is all so very good.

Please enjoy the Christmas holiday season and the spirit of giving, no matter your religious faith. Sacred as it is to celebrate the birth of Jesus Christ, the holiday season is uniquely American, bringing together people of all faiths and economic circumstances. Whether it's a present, a charitable gift, or a friendly gesture to a passerby, Santa lives on. Although the days are short and the nights are long, it is the most wonderful time of the year.

Sources of Inspiration

www.History.com

www.Wikipedia.com

Ayers, D., Balogh, B., Connolly, N., and Freeman, J. *Backstory Podcast*, Virginia Humanities.

Biewen, J. *Seeing White, Scene on Radio Podcast*, Center for Documentary Studies, Duke University. (2017).

Haidt, J. *The Happiness Hypothesis: Finding Truth in Ancient Wisdom.* New York: Basic Books. (2006).

L. Frank Baum. *The Wonderful Wizard of Oz.* (1900). Illustrated by W. W. Denslow.

The National Archives website: https://www.archives.gov/founding-docs/declaration-transcript

Rubin, G. *The Happiness Project.* UK: HarperCollins. (2009).

The Sacred Pipe: Black Elk's Account of the Seven Rites of the Oglala Sioux, as told to Joseph Epes Brown. University of Oklahoma Press. (1953).

Appendix

Declaration of Independence

In Congress, July 4, 1776

The unanimous Declaration of the thirteen United States of America,

When, in the Course of human events, it becomes necessary for one people to dissolve the political bonds which have connected them with another, and to assume among the powers of the earth, the separate and equal station to which the Laws of Nature and of Nature's God entitle them, a decent respect to the opinions of mankind requires that they should declare the causes which impel them to the separation.

We hold these truths to be self-evident, that all men are created equal, that they are endowed by their Creator with certain unalienable Rights, that among these are Life, Liberty and the pursuit of Happiness. --That to secure these rights, Governments are instituted among Men, deriving their just powers from the consent of the governed. --That whenever any Form of Government becomes destructive to these ends, it is the Right of the People to alter or to abolish it, and to institute new Government, laying its foundation on such principles and organizing its powers in such form, as to them shall seem most likely to affect their Safety and Happiness. Prudence, indeed, will dictate that Governments long established should not be changed for light and transient causes; and accordingly all experience hath shown that mankind are more disposed to suffer, while evils are sufferable, than to right themselves by abolishing the forms to which they are accustomed. But when a long train of abuses and usurpations, pursuing invariably the same Object evinces a design to reduce them under absolute Despotism, it is their right, it is their duty, to throw off such Government, and to provide new Guards for their future security. --Such has been the patient sufferance of these Colonies; and such is now the necessity which constrains them to alter their former Systems of Government. The history of the present King of Great Britain is a history of repeated injuries and usurpations, all having in direct object the establishment of an absolute Tyranny over these States. To prove this, let Facts be submitted to a candid world.

He has refused his Assent to Laws, the most wholesome and necessary for the public good.

He has forbidden his Governors to pass Laws of immediate and pressing importance, unless suspended

Appendix

in their operation till his Assent should be obtained; and when so suspended, he has utterly neglected to attend to them.

He has refused to pass other Laws for the accommodation of large districts of people, unless those people would relinquish the right of Representation in the Legislature, a right inestimable to them and formidable to tyrants only.

He has called together legislative bodies at places unusual, uncomfortable, and distant from the depository of their public Records, for the sole purpose of fatiguing them into compliance with his measures.

He has dissolved Representative Houses repeatedly, for opposing with manly firmness his invasions on the rights of the people.

He has refused for a long time, after such dissolutions, to cause others to be elected; whereby the Legislative powers, incapable of Annihilation, have returned to the People at large for their exercise; the State remaining in the meantime exposed to all the dangers of invasion from without, and convulsions within.

He has endeavored to prevent the population of these States; for that purpose obstructing the Laws for Naturalization of Foreigners; refusing to pass others to encourage their migration hither, and raising the conditions of new Appropriations of Lands.

He has obstructed the Administration of Justice, by refusing his Assent to Laws for establishing Judiciary powers.

He has made Judges dependent on his Will alone for the tenure of their offices and the amount and payment of their salaries.

He has erected a multitude of New Offices and sent hither swarms of Officers to harass our people and eat out their substance.

He has kept among us, in times of peace, Standing Armies without the consent of our Legislature.

He has affected to render the Military independent of and superior to Civil power.

He has combined with others to subject us to a jurisdiction foreign to our constitution, and unacknowledged by our laws; giving his Assent to their Acts of pretended Legislation:

For Quartering large bodies of armed troops among us:

For protecting them, by mock Trial, from punishment for any Murders which they should commit on the Inhabitants of these States:

For cutting of our Trade with all parts of the world:

For imposing Taxes on us without our Consent:

Appendix

For depriving us in many cases of the benefits of Trial by Jury:

For transporting us beyond Seas to be tried for pretended offenses:

For abolishing the free System of English Laws in a neighboring Province, establishing therein an Arbitrary government, and enlarging its Boundaries so as to render it at once an example and fit instrument for introducing the same absolute rule in these Colonies:

For taking away our Charters, abolishing our most valuable Laws, and altering fundamentally the Forms of our Governments:

For suspending our own Legislatures, and declaring themselves invested with power to legislate for us in all cases whatsoever.

He has abdicated Government here, by declaring us out of his Protection and waging War against us.

He has plundered our seas, ravaged our Coasts, burned our towns, and destroyed the lives of our people.

He is at this time transporting large Armies of foreign Mercenaries to complete the works of death, desolation and tyranny, already begun with circumstances of Cruelty & perfidy scarcely paralleled in the most barbarous ages, and totally unworthy the Head of a civilized nation.

He has constrained our fellow Citizens taken Captive on the high Seas to bear Arms against their Country, to become the executioners of their friends and Brethren, or to fall themselves by their Hands.

He has excited domestic insurrections amongst us, and has endeavored to bring on the inhabitants of our frontiers, the merciless Indian Savages, whose known rule of warfare, is undistinguished destruction of all ages, sexes and conditions.

In every stage of these Oppressions we have Petitioned for Redress in the most humble terms: Our repeated Petitions have been answered only by repeated injury. A Prince, whose character is thus marked by every act which may define a Tyrant, is unfit to be the ruler of a free people.

Nor have We been wanting in attention to our British brethren. We have warned them from time to time of attempts by their legislature to extend an unwarrantable jurisdiction over us. We have reminded them of the circumstances of our emigration and settlement here. We have appealed to their native justice and magnanimity, and we have conjured them by the ties of our common kindred to disavow these usurpations, which would inevitably interrupt our connections and correspondence. We must, therefore, acquiesce in the necessity, which denounces our Separation, and hold them, as we hold the rest of mankind, Enemies in War, in Peace Friends.

Appendix

We, therefore, the representatives of the United States of America, in General Congress, assembled, appealing to the Supreme Judge of the world for the rectitude of our intentions, do, in the Name, and by the Authority of the good People of these Colonies, solemnly publish and declare, That these united colonies are, and of right ought to be Free and Independent States; that they are Absolved from all Allegiance to the British Crown, and that all political connection between them and the State of Great Britain, is and ought to be totally dissolved; and that as Free and Independent States, they have full Power to levy War, conclude Peace, contract Alliances, establish Commerce, and to do all other Acts and Things which Independent States may of right do. And for the support of this Declaration, with a firm reliance on the protection of divine Providence, we mutually pledge to each other our Lives, our Fortunes and our sacred Honor.

www.ingramcontent.com/pod-product-compliance
Lightning Source LLC
Chambersburg PA
CBHW070909080526
44589CB00013B/1235